Friedrich von Arentschildt, Frederick Cavendish Ponsonby

Instructions for officers and non-commissioned officers of

cavalry,

On outpost duty / By Lieut.-Colonel Von Arentschildt, First Hussars King's

German legion: with an abridgment of them by Lieut.-Colonel the Hon. F.

Ponsonby

Friedrich von Arentschildt, Frederick Cavendish Ponsonby

Instructions for officers and non-commissioned officers of cavalry,
On outpost duty / By Lieut.-Colonel Von Arentschildt, First Hussars King's German legion; with an abridgment of them by Lieut.-Colonel the Hon. F. Ponsonby

ISBN/EAN: 9783337730390

Printed in Europe, USA, Canada, Australia, Japan

Cover: Foto ©ninafisch / pixelio.de

More available books at **www.hansebooks.com**

INSTRUCTIONS

FOR OFFICERS AND NON-COMMISSIONED OFFICERS OF CAVALRY,

ON

OUTPOST DUTY;

BY

LIEUT.-COLONEL VON ARENTSCHILDT,

First Hussars King's German Legion:

WITH

AN ABRIDGMENT OF THEM

BY

LIEUT.-COLONEL THE HON. F. PONSONBY,

Twelfth Light Dragoons.

———

J. W. RANDOLPH:
121 MAIN STREET, RICHMOND, VA.
1861.

OUTPOST DUTY.

I.

INSTRUCTIONS FOR OFFICERS AND NONCOMMISSIONED OFFICERS:

BY LIEUT.-COLONEL VON ARENTSCHILDT.

II.

AN ABRIDGMENT OF THE SAME:

BY LIEUTENANT-COLONEL THE HON. F. PONSONBY.

LIEUTENANT-COLONEL VON ARENTSCHILDT'S

INSTRUCTIONS ON

OUTPOST DUTY.

SECTION II.

MARCHING FOR HIS DESTINATION.

On the march to the spot where the Picquet is to be placed, the Officer must pay great attention in examining the country, and particularly observe the places where he would make a stand in case the Picquet should be attacked by the Enemy : for instance, behind a bridge, a ravine, between bogs, &c., in order to keep off the enemy as long as possible. This is of the utmost importance to give the Corps time to turn out. The Commander of a Picquet who retires with his men at full speed, and the Enemy at his heels, deserves the severest punishment; he must retire as slow as possible, and constantly skirmish.

SECTION III.

IF NO PICQUET WAS ON THE SPOT BEFORE.

By Day.

Being arrived at the spot chosen by himself, or pointed out to him, he forms his Picquet, and takes out as many men as he thinks he has occasion for as Videttes. To fix upon the number of Videttes, is much facilitated by riding on the top of a hill, and observing the number of roads and hills in front. With these Videttes he goes on, and places them in such a manner that every one of them is able to see individually what is coming towards the Picquet, as well as the neighbouring Videttes. The remainder of the Picquet dismounts in the mean time, with the exception of one Sentry, who is to be placed a little in advance. The bridles are not to be taken off. In placing the Videttes the Officer will have acquired a sufficient knowledge of the country to be able to judge whether any of them are superfluous, (which is much to be avoided, as men and horses are unnecessarily fatigued by it,) or whether there ought to be more. Two-thirds of the Picquet now unbridle : it is to be recollected that the whole of a Picquet should never unbridle. The Officer then reconnoitres the country. Every one ambitious to do his duty well will make a little sketch, in which the following are to be marked :

1. Roads ; 2. Rivers ; 3. Bridges and Fords ; 4. Morasses, cavities, hollow roads, and mountains ; 5. Wood ; 6. Towns, Villages and their distances.

If the Officer does not acquire such an exact knowledge of the country, he cannot be responsible for the security of his Picquet, and of the corps to which he belongs.

By this time he will have had opportunity to fix upon the spot where his Picquet and Videttes ought to be placed at night.

By Night.

It is impossible to lay down any fixed principles on this subject ; but the general rules are, to advance the Picquet at least two or three English miles in front of the main body : to place it behind a bridge, ravine, wood, or bog through which the road passes, in order to be enabled to make a stand immediately on being attacked, and to place Videttes in front and flanks. Small Patrols of two or three men in front, and flanks at half an hour's interval, and constantly kept in motion, will give perfect security, particularly if one of the men sometimes dismounts, and listens with his ear on the ground : he will hear the march of troops at a great distance. This precaution is indispensable in stormy weather. Upon coming by night to a new spot, particularly in a mountainous or woody country, small Patrols must be pushed forward immediately in all the roads, &c., to secure in the first instance the placing of Videttes, &c., &c.

If the enemy is near, no fire is to be lighted, and the spot where the Picquet stands should be changed very often ; one-half of the Picquet should be mounted, the other stand with the bridles in their hands.

SECTION IV.

RELIEVING ANOTHER PICQUET.

Great part of what is said in sections I. and II. is likewise to be applied here. As soon as the Officer is arrived at the Picquet that is to be relieved, he forms at its left flank, or behind it, as the nature of the ground requires, draws out a non-commissioned officer, and as many Videttes as he has to relieve, (the remainder dismounts,) and proceeds with the Officer commanding the old Picquet and his own non-commissioned Officer to relieve the Videttes. The Officers should be very particular in delivering the detail of their duties, and the following is to be observed on such occasions.

1. All written orders or instructions must be delivered, and the verbal orders written down and signed by the Officer who is relieved.

2. The outlines of the sketch belonging to the Officer commanding the old Picquet are to be copied and filled up afterwards—

3. To whom the reports are to be sent.

4. Where the Picquets on the flanks are stationed; what roads lead to them; how often Patrols are exchanged between them in the night. In case the roads to them are little known, or difficult to be found, the Non-commissioned Officer of the old Picquet must show them to that of the new one, who takes another man with him.

5. Inquiries must be made as to the knowledge the Officer has of the enemy, particularly where he patrols to ; whether he thinks that the Picquet has been well posted, at night as well as in the day, or whether improvements can be made. If such an improvement is found to be necessary by placing one or two more Videttes, they ought to be posted immediately, but the same is to be reported without delay.

At the relief of the Videttes, both the officers of the old and new Picquets should be present. They must listen to the delivery of instructions from the old Vidette to the new one, and the latter is to be desired to repeat what has been delivered to him, to prevent any mistake. The principal points of these instructions should be : on what roads and from what part of the country the enemy may be expected to advance ; where the neighbouring Videttes are stationed, in order to be able to repeat their signals, which they may have particular orders to make. The new Vidette must be very particular in occupying the same spot that the old one did, as sometimes the difference of one yard may be of great consequence in observing or being observed at a great distance.

If the relief is not made with the above-mentioned exactness, all orders that have been issued may be misunderstood or quite forgotten in the course of two or three days.

After all the Videttes have been relieved in this manner, the spot where the Picquet and

Videttes have been stationed in the night are to be pointed out to the Officer of the new Picquet.

The old Picquet now marches off, and the new one takes its place. The horses may be then unbridled, except one-third or one-fourth.

SECTION V.

DURING HIS STAY ON PICQUET.

By Day.

A Dismounted Sentry who is able to see the movements of the several Videttes, and who can acquaint the Picquet with them, is a measure so necessary for the safety of the Picquet, that it never ought to be omitted.

One-third or one-fourth of the horses are always bridled up and ready to advance; the men must never take off their swords and belts; one-half of them may sleep in the middle of the day, the other in the afternoon, that they may be all perfectly alert at night.

The men must not be allowed to go into houses or villages in the neighbourhood; such straggling leads to irregularities, and on being rapidly attacked by the enemy the horses will be lost.

When the men water their horses, they must bridle them up, and take everything with them; none but inexperienced and negligent Officers will allow the men to water their horses at any distance with merely the halter on, and leaving the bridle with the Picquet.

In short, a Picquet must at all times be ready for an attack in half a minute.

How often the Picquets are to patrol, where to and how far, is generally ordered by the Officer commanding the outposts. If there are no orders upon these subjects, the following Patrols will be sent:

The first at half an hour before day-break, or so early that it has time to arrive at the place of its destination at daylight; here it will remain until it is full day-light. Whoever leads the Patrol is to go up on the top of a hill, where he can look about to a considerable distance, and then he returns, the second Patrol at ten o'clock; the third at two o'clock; the fourth towards evening; the fifth at midnight.

This arrangement, however, depends upon the distance of the enemy, except the morning Patrol before day-light, which is to go under all circumstances.

It cannot be too frequently told to all Patrols, that they are often to look to the rear when they return. The Enemy very frequently succeeds in following a negligent Patrol of this kind, and surprising the Picquet, which thinks itself perfectly secure. In a close country it is very advisable after the return of a patrol, to send forward again a few men at the distance of a mile, to be certain that the Enemy did not follow the Patrol.

By Night.

The proper time for the Picquet to go to the night post is when it gets too dark for the day Videttes to see at any distance; they are then called in, and the position for the night is taken up.

If there are any apprehensions of being betrayed to the enemy by spies or inhabitants of the country, it is advisable to change the spot again, but the Videttes will remain.

In case the enemy is very near, the Picquet must be mounted; this is, however, very fatiguing for men and horses; it is, therefore, better to cause one-third or one-half to mount and to advance about a hundred yards; the remainder is to stand by their horses.

At night the Videttes may be relieved every hour. The Relief should ride along the chain of Videttes; this may be considered, at the same time, as a visiting Patrol. Besides this Patrol, the Videttes are to be visited every half hour to be quite sure that none of them have deserted or fallen asleep. If the enemy is near, the Videttes should be all double; which is at all times to be recommended in preference to single Videttes, if the strength of the Picquet will allow it.

In case a man deserts, the spot where the Picquet is stationed ought to be instantly changed to some hundred yards' distance, and the fire to be extinguished; the Videttes are to be made acquainted with this change, and double attention paid. In such cases double Videttes patrol among themselves in the following manner:

Fig. I.

1	2	3	4	5	6
......0	0.........0		0.........0	0.........

Videttes.

No. 1 patrols to his left, and when returned No. 2 proceeds to No. 3, and returns to his station: No. 3 patrols to No. 2, and when returned, No. 4 will go to No. 5 and return; 5 and 6, and all the other Videttes do the same. If this is done it is impossible that anything can pass unperceived. The desertion of any man must be reported without delay.

When the Enemy is close, the following measures not only contributes to insure security, but is the best way to learn when the Enemy is on the move: A few men are to patrol during the night every hour beyond the chain of Videttes, in different directions, and to go as close to the Enemy as they can, unperceived. As soon as they are far enough, one man dismounts and listens with his ear on the ground; he will be enabled to hear at a considerable distance when Troops march. This undoubtedly gives security to the outpost; but it is particularly recommended, being the only means to ascertain the secret movements of the enemy in the night, to discover which the greatest exertions ought to be made, as it is of the utmost importance to the

Commander-in-chief to be immediately acquainted with them.

The Picquets have frequently no orders to de-
tain people that pass through the line of outposts
towards the enemy ; but in the evening and during the night every one attempting to do so
must remain with the Picquet until daylight.
Persons suspected of carrying any papers with
them are to be searched, and sent to the Commanding Officer, with a written statement why
they appear suspicious. Half an hour before
daylight the morning Patrols will be sent on the
roads in front, and as soon as it is quite light the
Picquet and Videttes take up their position for
the day.

SECTION VI.

PLACING OF VIDETTES.

Although little can be said upon this subject, (everything depending upon the nature of
the country,) the following rules may be applicable :

By Day.

They are generally placed upon hills, to enable them to have a good view of everything in
front. In a mountainous country the ravines
and narrow valleys now and then cannot be observed at the top of a hill ; in this case a Vidette
is to be placed in the bottom. It is desirable to
place the Videttes on the top of hills, near a tree

or large stone, to prevent the enemy from seeing them, as he may conclude, by seeing one of them, what position the whole line of Videttes and Picquets, and even sometimes the corps to which they belong, have taken up.

When the Videttes are placed in such a manner that they can overlook their front, see each other and the ground between them, so that nothing can pass unperceived, they are placed as they ought to be.

In order to spare men and horses, no more Videttes than necessary are to be out.

In a thick fog the Videttes stationed at a considerable distance on the flanks are taken off the hills and placed on more suitable spots. The country may require that the position fixed upon for the night should be taken up during the day, in which case the country in front must be continually scoured in all directions by small Patrols; which measure always gives sufficient security.

By Night.

The Videttes are taken off the hills, and placed on the roads, behind fords, bridges, ravines, &c., by which the enemy may approach the Picquet. At a clear moonshine they ought to be near a tree or bush, to prevent their being seen by the enemy, as in a close country it may happen that he approaches them unperceived, notwithstanding all their attention. They should be placed at the bottom of a hill, so that any object moving on the top would be easily perceived even in the darkest night.

They are by no means to be advanced further than that their firing can be distinctly heard by the Picquet, even in a stormy night.

SECTION VII.

INSTRUCTIONS FOR THE VIDETTES,

And what the Officer Commanding the Picquet has to observe on their making Signals.

By Day.

1. When a Vidette discovers anything suspicious on the side of the enemy, should it be a rising dust or the glittering of arms, he should move his horse in a circle at a walk. The Officer should instantly proceed to the Vidette, accompanied by a corporal and four men, and if he cannot distinctly discover by his spy-glass the cause of the dust, he should send off the men that accompanied him, as a Patrol, or go himself; so far that he can report in case he sees Troops, how strong they are, whether consisting of Cavalry, Infantry, or Artillery, but particularly in which direction they march. This report must be dispatched in writing, without the least delay.

The Commander of a Picquet should never omit to report occurrences of this kind, although they may have no connexion with the security of his Picquet. Patrols and Picquets must always report the movements of any body of Troops, even of a small number.

2. If the Videttes observe Troops marching towards them, but yet at a great distance, they will ride the circle in a trot. The Officer's duty is, as in 1.

3. If the enemy's Troops come towards the Picquet, and are at only one English mile distance from it, the Videttes circle in a gallop. The Officer immediately advances with his whole Picquet. His duty is prescribed in the paragraph on the Attack of a Picquet.

If the enemy is so near that the Videttes are obliged to gallop to their Picquets for their own security, they fire their carbines and pistols in case the Picquet should not have advanced.

By Night.

1. As soon as the Videttes hear a suspicious noise, even at a great distance, such as the rattling of carriages or artillery, the barking of dogs in the villages in front, or if they observe any fire, one of the Videttes must instantly report it to the Officer of the Picquet, in order that the circumstances may be inquired into by a Patrol.

2. Should any person approach the Vidette, he must be challenged with " Who comes there?" so loud that the Picquet and the next Videttes are able to hear it. If those that approach do not halt upon this, the Vidette should challenge a second time ; if they do not halt, he should fire, and retire

on the road pointed out to him, &c., &c. But if those that he challenged halt, he cries out "One man dismount!" and at the same time, "Sergeant advance!" The dismounted man he desires to approach, but not nearer than three yards, and holds the cocked pistol directed against him. The Officer of the Picquet must be instantly there, and examine carefully where the person or persons came from, who sent them, and what for, (when the enemy has the intention to surprise a Picquet, he sometimes pretends to be a friendly Patrol,) to what regiment they belong, the name of their Brigadier, Commanding Officer and Captains—where their regiment is encamped, &c., &c.; if they are able readily and justly to answer these questions, they may pass unmolested, as in that case one may consider it a certainty that they are no enemies.

SECTION VIII.

ON THE ARRIVAL OF A FLAG OF TRUCE.

Any person coming from the enemy with a Flag of Truce, must never be allowed to advance further than the chain of Videttes. When a Vidette makes the signal, the Officer of the Picquet meets the Flag of Truce with four men, and desires the bearer of it to halt, if possible in a bottom, or makes him face towards the side he came from, as it may be only the intention of the enemy to make observations respecting our position, or to see how the Picquet is placed, in order to surprise it in the night. Does the bearer of the Flag of Truce only bring letters, they are to be taken from him, and a receipt given for them; if he insists upon being allowed to proceed, permission must be asked, which being obtained, the person proceeding is blindfolded; a Non-commissioned Officer leads his horse, and brings him to the General's quarter. Should there be more persons than one, the remainder must stay where they are, until the other returns. A Flag of Truce ought to be treated with the utmost politeness; if refreshments can be given, it is desirable to do so; but no conversation relative to our position and to the army is to be permitted.

After a Flag of Truce has left the Videttes, the Picquet must be very attentive.

SECTION IX.

DESERTERS COMING FROM THE ENEMY.

At Daytime.

As they are discernable at a distance, but cannot be known to be deserters, a proportionate number from the Picquet must already have advanced to the line of Videttes when they approach. Deserters generally make themselves known by flourishing the cap about their head, and calling out "Deserter!" But this is not to be depended upon; their further behaviour must be previously observed. They are to be told that it is an order in the army to take their arms from them—that is to say, their swords: the flints are only taken off the fire-arms. In proportion to their number they are then to be brought to the General's quarter by one, two, or three men, and their swords returned to them.

Whenever any property is taken from a deserter, the act is always to be severely punished.

At Night.

Great caution is to be used in this instance. The Videttes must order them to halt at some distance, and by no means allow them to come too near. The Picquet advances, and the Deserters are to come towards it one by one, and be disarmed immediately. After all this is done, they are brought to the rear. Deserters must be examined respecting the movements, &c., of the Enemy.

SECTION X.

WHEN THE PICQUET IS ATTACKED.

By Day.

The first to be done is to report what is going on, and in a mountainous and woody country at the same time to acquaint the Picquets on the flanks with it. After this the Picquet advances, but in such a manner that it cannot be cut off, and begins to skirmish. It will seldom be practicable or suitable to advance farther than the chain of Videttes. Is the Officer obliged to retire, it must be done as slow as possible, to gain time for the Corps to turn out.   If the Commander of the Picquet has previously fixed upon places where to make a stand, as prescribed in Section II., it is now time to make use of them, when he has retired so far.   The best way for cavalry to defend a bridge, ravine, or ford, is the following (fig. 2) :

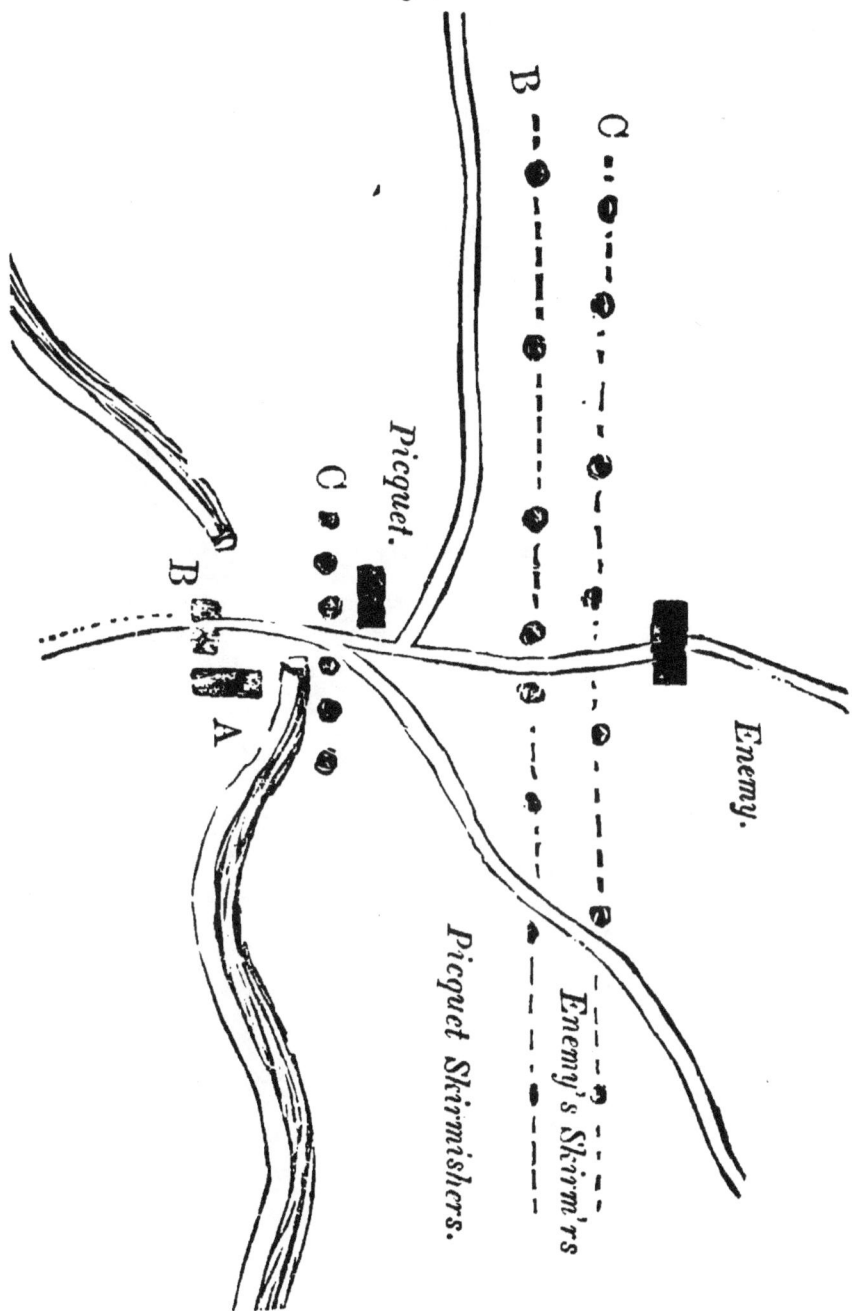

Fig. 2.

When the Picquet has been obliged to retire three or four hundred yards to the bridge, the Officer is to gallop over it with the same, and to post himself in A, as close as possible, with his right flank on it, leaving the passage open. As soon as his skirmishers see that he has taken up his position, and that the passage over the bridge is open, they likewise gallop over it, and face about again in B. The Enemy will certainly halt, and if he pushes on, those in A have only to cut him down as he is not in a state of defence, being obliged to expose his left flank: those in B charge likewise, or fire upon him at eight yards' distance. In this manner the Enemy must halt, and is obliged to retire a little, in order to throw skirmishers in C, to drive away the Picquet by their fire. However, time is gained by this, on which sometimes the honor and welfare of the Corps depend. This consideration only could induce me to be so circumstantial upon this subject.

When the Picquets on the flanks are not attacked at the same time, they can be sometimes of service in acting upon the Enemy's flanks; yet the nature of the ground must not endanger them to be cut off. But however favorable the ground may often be, it appears sometimes surprising to see that the nearest Picquets frequently do not undertake anything on such occasions, and behave exactly as if the whole business did not concern them at all.

In general, it is a rule that the Picquets that

are not attacked, retire in a line with those engaged.

By Night.

It is mentioned in Section VII. that when the Videttes have fired their fire-arms, they must gallop back by the road pointed out to them. It is of the hightest importance to instruct the night Videttes, that, in case the Enemy should rapidly attack them, they are not to retire towards the Picquet, but a hundred and fifty yards to the right or left of it, firing constantly in the meantime, and trying by these means to mislead the Enemy, and draw him after them. The Picquet hereby gains time to mount, and to fall in the Enemy's flank and rear, with a great noise, who will certainly suspect to have fallen in an ambush, be puzzled, and perhaps lose some prisoners. Immediately after this attack is made, it will be best to fall back again on the road fixed upon for a retreat. It is therefore necessary to show the men in the day the road which the Videttes are to take, when they are attacked in the night, and likewise whereabout they are to rejoin the Picquet. The other part of the retreat is nearly the same as in the day, with this difference only, that there cannot be skirmishers in front, but only two or three men at the head. It is necessary to fire as much as possible, but wherever a stand can be made, an obstinate defence is desirable. It is unnecessary to remark that a report is to be sent as soon as attacked.

II. ADVANCED GUARD.

By Day.

Fig. 3.

Suppose the same consists of one Officer, two Non-commissioned officers, and twenty-four men, the officer commanding tells them off as in fig. 3.

This gives an extension of 1,500 yards, which is sufficient for twenty-four men. If the column is larger, the Advanced Guard is likewise stronger and more extended. A rule is, that the Advanced Guard should take up so much ground, that when it discovers the enemy, the column has sufficient time to form and make dispositions, either for attacking or retiring. The several divisions of the Advanced Guard must always keep their support in sight, and be careful to preserve the same distances. When the column halts, the Advanced Guard does the same, but the three men at the head instantly occupy the neighbouring heights, in case the enemy should be within four or five hundred yards.

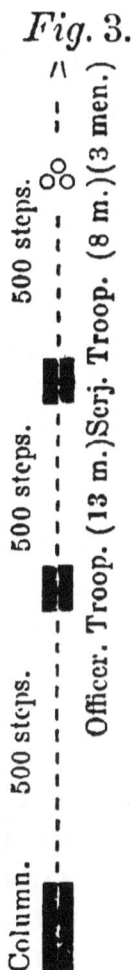

500 steps. 500 steps. 500 steps. Column.

(3 men.) Serj. Troop. (8 m.) Officer. Troop. (13 m.)

If the Advanced Guard comes to a wood which is supposed to be 2,000 yards broad, the Sergeant reinforces the three men at the head with six more, who extend themselves so far to the right and left as to be in line with the first three, that they can see each other, and what is concealed between them, and he follows with the two men left him, the three men in advance on the road. Should the wood be too large, the Officer must send two men to the right, and as many to the left, round it, who are carefully to examine whether they can see the traces of troops marched into the wood, which is to be immediately reported. The column halts until this is ascertained.

Generally only two men march at the heads, but this is wrong ; there ought to be three, whose duty is the following : Is a height in front, the centre man of the three trots on until he can look over it; if there is one to the right or left of the road, one of the other two men does the same. Near an enemy this must always be done, supposed even that the hill is 1500 or 2000 yards distance. Men that go on the top of a hill to reconnoitre in this manner, (they may belong to an Advanced Guard or a Patrol,) must proceed more carefully than is generally done. As a great deal depends upon seeing the Enemy, and not to be seen by him, they must, when nearly on the top of the hill, take off the cap, and only go as high as just to be able to look over ; this produces the great advantage, that the Com-

manding Officer may observe the marching Enemy, and make his arrangements accordingly for
a retreat, an attack, or an ambuscade. All these
advantages are lost when the Enemy discovers
us.

Should the march be directed towards a village, one man goes round it to the right, the other to the left, and the third through it, if the sit-
uation of the village permits to do so. The
Non-Commissioned Officer of the Advanced
Guard also trots on until he arrives near the village, and reinforces the men going through it
with three more ; one of these four men goes to
the right, the other to the left, through the bye-
roads ; two men proceed through the middle of
it, at such a distance from each other, that the
hindmost always keep in sight the one before
him. Should these men in patrolling the village
find no inhabitants, they are to look into the
windows, ride into the yards, and examine carefully if perhaps the Enemy concealed himself ;
those going round the village look at the entrances to see if Troops marched into the village.
The Sergeant, with his men, follows slowly ;
when he has passed through the village he col-
lects his men, sends three men again at the head,
and reports to his Officer, who has halted behind
the village, that the same is patrolled, &c.

It is unnecessary to observe, that these and
other precautionary measures are not requisite
when the Enemy cannot be expected.

By Night.

The Advanced Guard is told off as by day, but the distances between the several divisions must not be as large. The Officer's Division is a hundred yards from the column, the Sergeant a hundred from the Officer's, and the head fifty from the Sergeant's party. Between these Divisions, single men are to ride, who can see each other, to prevent the communication being lost.

If an Advanced Guard is unexpectedly attacked during the night, or meets with the Enemy, it has no other choice but instantly to fall upon him. The Non-Commissioned Officer must be instructed to disperse, in such a case, to the right and left, and to fire as much as possible; but the Officer advances rapidly with his Division, and charges. This is the only way to give time to the column to prepare for an attack. It is an unpardonable fault in an Advanced Guard to be frightened, and to retire upon the column, every thing will then be in confusion, and it would have been better, if there had been no Advanced Guard at all ; but if it advanced with intrepidity the column has time.

Should the Advanced Guard be obliged, by a superior force, to retire, after having fought bravely, this retreat ought to be made on either side of the Column, but never on the Column, because the latter would be fired upon, and the confusion increased.

On all these subjects the men should be previ-

ously well instructed. Every Commanding Officer of a detached party must consider it as one
of his first duties to give clear and circumstantial
instructions to his men, without which they will
frequently act contrary to his ideas, even with
the best intention.

B

Fig. 4.

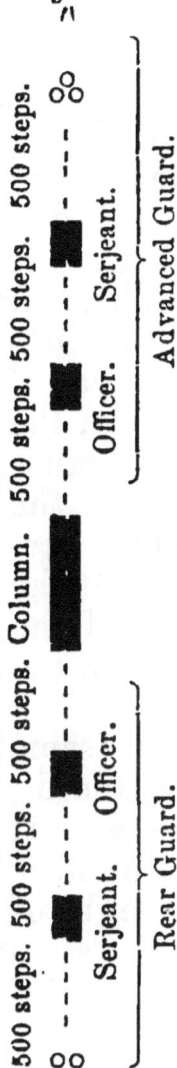

Is told off in separate divisions, the same as an Advance Guard, only in reverse order (fig. 4.)

The object of a Rear Guard is to prevent the enemy's approaching the column unperceived; two men in the Rear are sufficient, but these must be picked men. When the march is undisturbed, they often halt on the heights so as just to be able to look over to the rear, to discover the enemy. When a mountain is near, the Officer will do well to ride on the top of it, and to look about the country with his spyglass.

If the enemy follows closely with a few men, to see the strength of our column, it is to be tried to lead them into an ambuscade, and to make prisoners, or to drive them off. But in case the Rear is attacked, it is instantly to be supported by the Serjeant's Troop, and this by the Officer's Troop, which both immediately advance for that purpose, in order not to allow the enemy to come too near

B2

the Column. The Commanding Officer of the Column will then support him, or give directions to retire slowly. If the enemy follows with a more considerable force, suppose one squadron, *without* attacking, the Rear Guard will follow the Column in the subsequent manner. When the Column is a thousand yards distant from the Officer's Troop, he trots on to the ordinary distance of five hundred yards, halts, and fronts ; as soon as the Serjeant sees that the Officer has fronted, he trots on to five hundred yards' distance from the Officer, and fronts likewise, the two men in the rear trot on to the same distance from the Serjeant's Troop. In this manner the Rear alternately follows the Column, which prevents the enemy from coming too near; at the same time an engagement is avoided, and the horses saved. Whenever the Column halts, the different parties face towards the enemy.

At night, the Rear Guard behaves in the same manner as prescribed for the Advanced Guard ; that is to say, the intervals between the several Troops are to be shorter, and a sufficient number of single men placed in them not to lose sight of the Column and each other.

IV. PATROLS.

SECTION I.

SIDE PATROLS.

Fig. 5.

Patrols are detached on the Flanks, when the enemy can disturb the Flanks of the column. They are placed in the following manner (fig. 5):

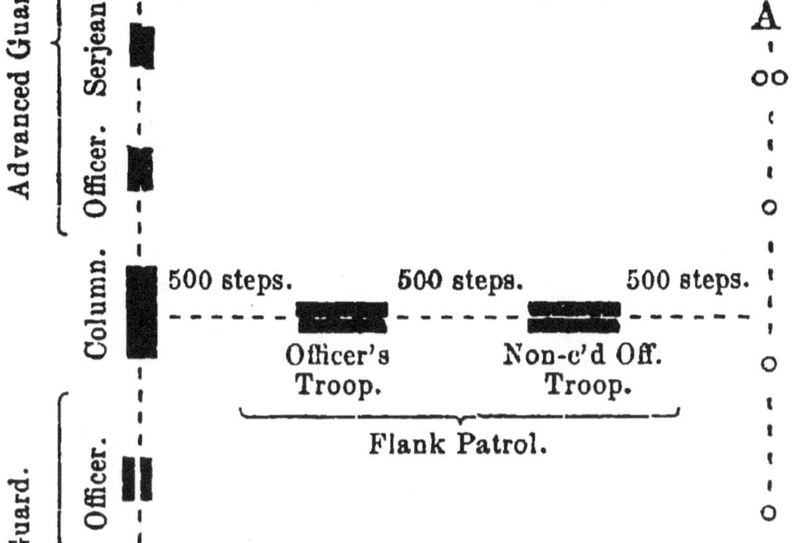

The two men in A must not only from time to time communicate with the Advanced Guard—that is to say, one of them incline to the left until he can see

B3

it—but the other, when there is a height near, even at a thousand yards' distance, must ride so far on the top of it that he can look over. When attacked, Side Patrols behave as Advanced and Rear Guards. They meet the enemy, and do not suffer him to come too near the Column.

When a Side Patrol meets with a wood in the direction of its march, the disposition is altered (fig. 6).

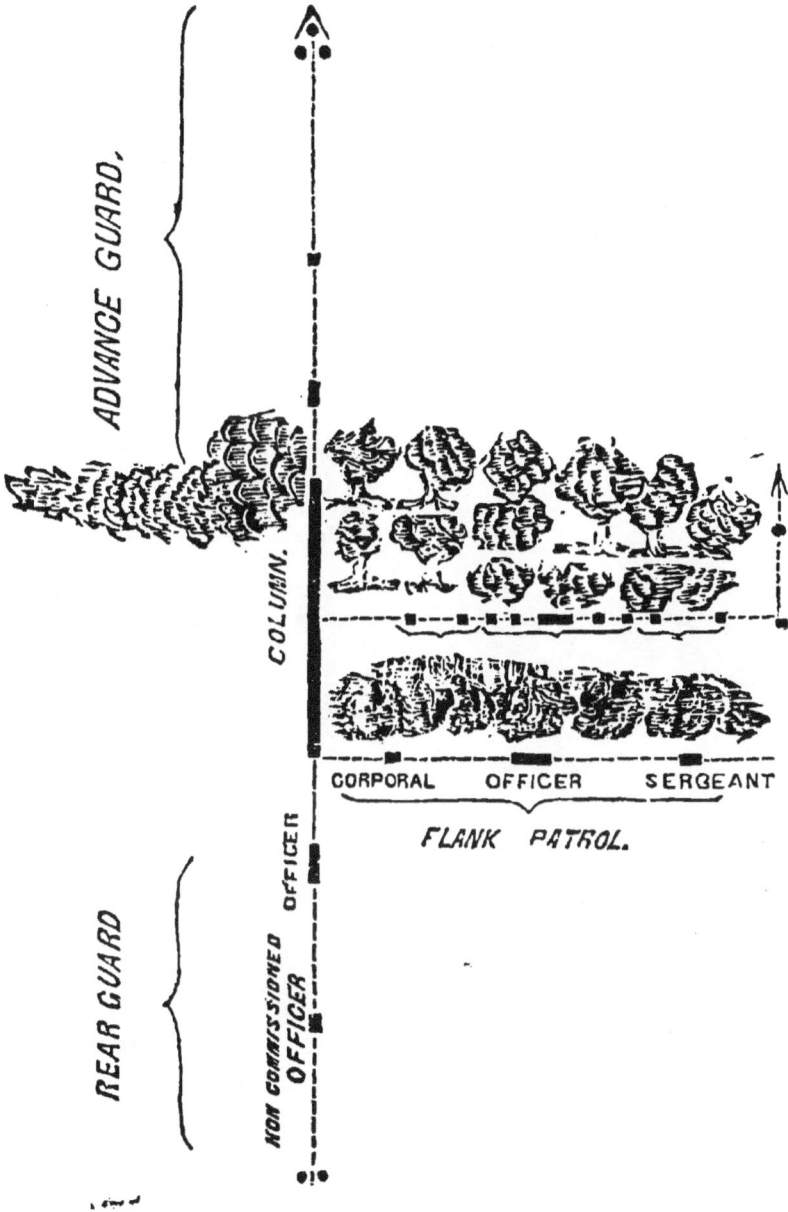

Fig. 6.

ADVANCE GUARD.

REAR GUARD

COLUMN.

NON COMMISSIONED OFFICER

OFFICER

CORPORAL   OFFICER   SERGEANT

FLANK PATROL.

The officer detaches the Serjeant's Troop to the right, the Corporal's and four men to the left, and himself remains with his men in the centre. The Serjeant sends two men to the skirts of the wood : these must look at the tracks, and one of them ride on a height, if any is near; the remainder divide themselves to the left of these two men, at such a distance that they can keep each other in sight. The Corporal divides his men in the same manner from the Right Flank of the Column to the Officer's Troop. If the Officer perceives that these two lines are not extensive enough to cover the ground towards his Troop, he detaches a sufficient number of men to the right and left to form a perfect line, which line must be careful never to get at the head of the Column. The Non-commissioned officers endeavor to keep their men in the same line with the Officer's Division.

It sometimes excites pity to see the men unnecessarily gallop and fatigue their horses on such occasions, only from want of instructions, without doing more good than they would have done at a walk.

SECTION II.

PATROLLING A WOOD.

This is done in the same manner as if (Section I.,) a Side Patrol meets with a wood, with the difference that two men are likewise sent round to the left extremity of the wood.

SECTION III.

PATROLS OF DISCOVERY

Consists generally of a pretty considerable force, to be enabled to defend themselves against a small hostile party or patrol, and are sent for the purpose of ascertaining whether a certain place is in the Enemy's possession, whether he is on the move against us, or whether a certain district is occupied by him. Such a Patrol marches, after having passed the chain of Videttes, with the ordinary precautions of having three men for Advanced, and two for Rear Guard, and sends, in case the country requires it, one man to the right, and another to the left, on the heights.

As not unfrequently the safety, but also the attainment of the object for which the Patrol was sent out, depends upon its not being seen by the Enemy, before the Patrol has discovered him, it is of the utmost importance to instruct the men at the head very accurately, they must not merely be satisfied with looking before them, but look at the tracks of the cross-roads very minutely, and mount every hill with caution, &c.

If this is done, the Patrol will sometimes have opportunities to make prisoners. When a Patrol sees the Enemy advance towards it with not too strong a force, it must try to conceal itself and rapidly attack the unsuspecting enemy: he will get into confusion, fly, and perhaps lose some prisoners. If the Enemy has been discovered before, but is too strong, the Patrol retires: is perhaps not seen by him at all ; and circumstances may allow that it is able to continue its march, and to obtain the object of its first destination. All these advantages are lost when the Enemy discovers it.

A Patrol must never enter a village or wood until it has been explored ; but this is to be managed in such a way that the Patrol is not delayed : for the leader of it must not forget that the Officer who sent him out calculates the time of his return: if he does not come back near that time, he that sent him will get apprehensive, and send another Patrol after him, whereby men and horses are fatigued, which would have been avoided had the Leader of the Patrol been active in the performance of his duty.

If a village is to be passed at night, which the Enemy can be expected to have occupied, the Patrol is to halt (about five or six hundred yards) on the side of it. When no Videttes of the Enemy are visible, a few men are sent to the right and left, who approach gradually to ascertain whether the entrances of the village are occupied by Infantry, and to try to find an inhabitant, whom they bring to the Patrol, or listen whether they can hear anything. If nothing can be learned by these means, the Patrol proceeds with the same precautions as mentioned in a former Section.

If a Patrol is ordered to ascertain by night, whether and how a village is occupied, three of the best horses are to be picked out for the head, eight men are to follow at twenty-four yards' distance, and the remainder of the Patrol follows at a hundred yards' distance: in this manner the Enemy's Vidette must be approached, without the least noise; as soon as the Vidette challenges, the advance of the Patrol must go on at full speed to take him prisoner. Should they be unsuccessful in this, the eleven men, together rapidly attack the Picquet, to bring off a prisoner, with whom they retire. The alarm will be given in the village, to a certainty, and the sounding of a trumpet or the beating of drums will enable us to judge by what Troops it is occupied. If a Patrol goes so far that it is obliged to feed the horses, it should never be done in a village, but in an open country under some trees, and Videttes are to be placed during the time.

If it is necessary to get provisions and forage out of villages, they are to be brought out.

On such occasions, as on all others, the inhabitants are to be treated with politeness, and to rob them of anything deserves the severest punishment, and it is but natural if they betray such unpleasant guests to the Enemy.

If guides are required, or inquiries made after a road, more than one must be inquired after, to leave the people in uncertainty which road the Patrol means to take. Guides that are sent home are best to be led astray, by marching a wrong way until they are out of sight.

SECTION IV.

SECRET PATROLS.

These only consist of a few men, six or eight, and are generally sent on the flanks, and sometimes in the rear of the Enemy's Army, without the knowlege of the Enemy; are to go now and then at a great distance ; and are to remain for a considerable time, to make the necessary observations ; therefore this is the most difficult duty for Light Cavalry.

Many rules laid down for other Patrols are likewise here applicable.

A Patrol of this kind marches without Advanced and Rear Guard, and, if the country should require it, only one man rides on the heights without showing himself. If the Patrol proceeds so far, that it is obliged to march with great precaution, it must quit the great roads wherever it is possible, and take its march by bye-roads, deep valleys, &c., &c., to reach unseen the place of its destination. A Guide on horseback will be of great service to such a Patrol ; but he is to be paid for it, and treated well. When feeding the horses, it must go off the road into a bush or wood, and one man climbs up a tree to keep a look-out. If anything hostile approaches, the Patrol escapes without noise, and chooses another place of concealment until it can proceed by roundabout ways without danger. A fire can only be lighted with great caution, but it is better to avoid that entirely.   If an inhabitant accidentally meets with the Patrol at night, he must remain with it until the march is continued. Should a Secret Patrol be discovered by the Enemy, notwithstanding all precautions, it must fly ; as soon as the enemy gives up the pursuit, it must make attempts, by roundabout ways, to get notwithstanding, to the spot where its commission can be carried into execution.

This sometimes succeeds beyond expectation. A well-informed and clever officer is particularly required for this kind of duty ; who speaks the language of the country, and has a knowledge of the customs, habits, hopes, and fears of the inhabitants.   Such a one will be secure close to the Enemy, and be able to give the most certain and best intelligence.

It is to be remarked, that if the Leader of a Patrol, when returned, cannot answer the following questions about the roads he passed, viz :

Are they rocky, sandy, or boggy ?

How many rivers and rivulets he passed ; and the distances from one to the other ?

Are the banks of them bold, or only an impediment, &c. ?

How many bridges lead over them ? wooden or massive ?

Are fords beside those bridges, passable at every season for Cavalry, Infantry, or Artillery, &c. ?

How many villages are on the road, and what are

their names, and the distances from one to the other ?

Does the road go through wood ; or is it at some distance ; apparently how large, and what kind?

he has lost sight of a principal point of his duty.

The foregoing Instructions can only be considered as a sketch of the duties of the Light Cavalry. The young, yet inexperienced soldier may look upon it as an introduction to his duties ; he can only expect to acquire accomplishments by his own reflections and exertions.

AN ABRIDGMENT

OF

COLONEL ARENTSCHILDT'S

INSTRUCTIONS TO OFFICERS AND NON-COMMISSIONED
OFFICERS OF LIGHT CAVALRY;

BY

LIEUT.-COLONEL THE HON. F. PONSONBY,

Twelfth Light Dragoons.

INSTRUCTIONS

OFFICERS AND NON-COMMISSIONED OFFICERS OF CAVALRY, ON OUTPOST DUTY.

PICQUET.

I. The Officer commanding a Picquet should have the Names and Regiments of the men written down: he should inspect their arms and Ammunition; he should see that they are provided with Provisions and Forage, and should thoroughly understand the Orders which he receives.

2. On the march to where the Picquet is to be stationed, the country should be examined, and the places where a stand could be made in case the Picquet should be attacked, ought to be particularly observed. It is of the utmost importance to give the corps time to turn out, and the Commander of a Picquet who retires at full speed, with the Enemy at his heels, deserves the severest punishment. He must retire as slowly as possible, and constantly skirmish.

3. Upon arriving at the spot chosen for the Picquet, the Officer should ascertain the number

of Videttes necessary, by observing the roads and
hills in front ; he should then place them in such
a manner that they can each see what is coming
towards the Picquet, and at the same time observe one another. In the mean time the Picquet
should dismount, placing one Sentry a little in
advance ; and as soon as the Videttes are placed,
two-thirds of the Picquet may unbridle. The
Officer should make a little sketch, marking the
roads, rivers, bridges, or fords, morasses, cavities,
hollow roads, mountains, woods, towns, villages,
and their distances. An officer cannot feel confi-
dent for the security of his post, unless he has
acquired an exact knowledge of the country.

4. The principal rules for posting a Picquet at
night, are to advance it two or three miles in front
of the main body, behind a bridge, ravine, wood,
or bog, through which the road may pass, to place
Videttes in front, and on the flanks, and to send
out Patrols of two or three men each at half an
hour's interval. Sometimes a man should dismount and listen with his ear to the ground, by
which means he will hear the march of Troops at
a great distance. This precaution is necessary in
stormy weather. Upon coming by night to a
new spot, Patrols should be sent out in every direction before the Videttes are placed.

5. If the Enemy is near, no fire should be
lighted, the post should be frequently changed,
one-half of the Picquet should be mounted, one
hundred yards in advance, and the other half
should keep the bridles in their hands.

6. Upon relieving a Picquet, the new one should form in the rear of the old, the Videttes should be relieved, and the detail of duties should be thoroughly explained to the non-commissioned Officers and Privates. The Commander of the old Picquet should deliver over to the new one all written Orders, and the verbal Orders should be written down and signed by the Officer relieved : he should likewise inform him to whom reports are to be made, and give him every information he has relative to the Enemy, the Patrols, the Country, &c., and the night posts should be pointed out. At the relief of the Videttes, both officers of the old and new Picquet should be present, and listen to the instructions given by the old Vidette to the new one. These instructions should be from what part of the country the Enemy may be expected, where the neighbouring Videttes are stationed, in order to be able to repeat their signals. A Vidette should never move from the spot upon which he is placed, as the difference of a yard may prevent his observing, or being observed, at a great distance.

7. A dismounted Sentry should be placed in front of the Picquet, where he can observe the movements of the different Videttes. One-third of the horses must always be bridled up, and be ready to advance; the men must not take off their swords or belts; one-half may sleep in the middle of the day, the other half in the afternoon, so that they may be all perfectly alert at night. The men must not be allowed to leave the Picquet, or to

go into the villages, or houses, in the neighbor-hood. When the men water their horses, they must bridle them up, and take everything with them; in short, a Picquet must be always ready for an attack in half a minute.

PATROLS.

8. In sending out Patrols, the following Rules should be observed : The First should go out in the morning in time for it to arrive at its destination before daybreak, where it should remain until the Officer who commands it has had time to go to some rising ground and look over the country. The Second at Ten. The Third at Two. The Fourth towards Evening. And the Fifth at midnight. This arrangement, however, depends upon the distance of the Enemy, except the morning Patrol, which is to go under all circumstances. A Patrol, in returning, should look often to the rear, as the Enemy frequently succeeds in following a negligent Patrol. The Non-commissioned Officer should be particularly careful not to allow the men to fatigue their horses ; if it should be necessary to feed, it should never be done in a village, but in an open country, and a Vidette should be placed during the time. No man should be permitted to leave his horse for a moment, and any man who attempts to use an inhabitant of the country ill, or to take anything from the town by force, must be severely punished.

9. The time for the Picquet to go to the Night Post is when it becomes too dark for the Videttes to see at any distance. They are then called in, and the position for the night taken up. In case of any desertion, or that there are apprehensions of being betrayed to the enemy, by the inhabitants

or spies, the Picquet should change its ground, but the Videttes remain.

At night the Videttes must be relieved every hour and visited every half hour. The Videttes should at all times be double if possible. In foggy weather, and when it is very dark, the double Videttes should patrol among themselves, and communicate with one another. When the Enemy is near, the following measure contributes not only to security, but is the best method of knowing when the enemy is on the move: A few men should patrol during the night beyond the chain of Videttes in different directions, and as near the enemy as they can unperceived; they should then dismount and listen with the ear to the ground.

10. Every person attempting to pass the Outpost must be detained till the morning. After the morning Patrol has returned, or has reported that all is well, the Picquet should take up its position for the day.

11. Videttes should be placed by day on a high ground, so as to have an extensive view, but if possible near a rock or tree, so as not to be perceived by the Enemy; when the Videttes are placed in such a manner that they can overlook their front, see each other and the ground between them, so that nothing can pass unperceived, they are placed as they ought to be.

12. By night, Videttes are taken off the hills and placed on the roads, behind fords, bridges, ravines, &c.; they should be placed at the bot-

tom of hills, so that any object moving at the top would be easily perceived. They should by no means be advanced further than that their firing can be distinctly heard by the Picquet.

13. When a Vidette observes anything suspicious on the side of the Enemy, such as the glittering of arms, rising of dust, &c., he is to move his horse round in a circle at a walk ; the Officer should instantly proceed with a Corporal and four men to the Vidette ; and examine with his glass, or by a Patrol, thoroughly into the cause, after which he must make his report. If the Vidette observes Troops marching towards him, but at a great distance, he is to ride the circle in a trot ; the officer acts as in the former case. If the Enemy should approach the Vidette at no great distance, he is to ride the circle at a gallop. The Officer should advance with his whole Picquet ; his further duty is prescribed in Par. 15. If the Enemy is so near the Videttes that they are obliged to gallop to the Picquets for their own security, they should fire their Carbines or Pistols. By night, if the Videttes hear a suspicious noise, even at a great distance, such as the rattling of Carriages, barking of dogs, or if they observe any fire, one of them should instantly report the circumstances to the officer of the Picquet, in order that it may be inquired into by a Patrol. If any one should approach the Videttes, they must challenge, and desire the person or persons to halt till the Officer is informed. Should the person refuse to halt, being twice challenged in a

loud voice, the Vidette is to fire. Great caution must be observed by night if a Deserter should come from the Enemy, the Videttes must not let him approach too near; they must make him halt till the Officer comes up. By day, the Vidette is to make a signal to the sentry of the Picquet, should a Deserter approach, and a party will be immediately sent to receive him.

FLAG OF TRUCE.

14. No person coming from the Enemy with a Flag of Truce, is to be allowed to advance farther than the chain of Videttes. When the Vidette makes the signal, the Officer of the Picquet should meet the Flag of Truce with four more, and desire the bearer to halt, if possible, in a bottom, as the intention is frequently only to make observations on the position of the Picquet, in order to attack it at night. If the bearer only brings Letters, a receipt is to be given to the bearer and sent back ; but if he insists upon being allowed to proceed, further instructions must be obtained from the Officer commanding the Outposts. A Flag of Truce ought to be treated with the utmost civility, but no conversation relative to the Army is to be permitted.

15. When a Picquet is attacked, the Officer is immediately to communicate with the Picquets on his flank, and with the main body ; he is then to throw out his skirmishers, and if obliged to retire, it must be done as slowly as possible, to gain time for the corps to turn out. If the commander of the Picquet should have fixed upon places where to make a stand, (as recommended in Par. 2,) he will find the advantage ; if it be a bridge, ford, or ravine, he should act in the following manner: upon approaching the place, suppose a bridge, he should gallop over it with his Picquet, and form with his right flank to the

Enemy, taking care to leave the passage open. The skirmishers immediately after gallop over, and form directly fronting the passage of the bridge, and to the rear of the Picquet; the Enemy must necessarily halt, in order to drive the Picquet away by their fire; consequently, time is given to the main body, which is the grand object. If the Picquets on the flanks should not be attacked at the same time, they should endeavour, without exposing themselves to be cut off, to act upon the Enemy's flanks. In general, it is a rule for the Picquets not attacked to retire in a line with those engaged.

ADVANCED GUARD.

16. If an Officer, two non-commissioned Officers, and twenty-four Privates, form the Advanced Guard, the Officer should post himself about five hundred yards in front of the columns, with thirteen men, a serjeant and eight should be detached five hundred yards in advance of him, and three men five hundred yards in advance of the whole. The principle upon which an Advanced Guard, Rear Guard, or Side Patrol is sent out, is to give time to the column to make dispositions to attack or retreat, should an Enemy be discovered. The several divisions of the Advanced Guard must keep their support constantly in view, and if a wood, village, or ravine appear upon their front or flank, it must be carefully examined before the column proceeds: at night, the interval between the divisions of an Advance or Rear Guard, should be much less than during the day, and a communication should be kept up between the divisions, by two or three single men placed at such distances that they can see each other.

17. A great deal of responsibility is left to a non-commissioned Officer on outpost duty : he has frequently the command of Patrols, Picquets, &c.; it is therefore necessary for him to obtain a thorough knowledge of his duty. Unless he has authority to keep up the strictest discipline, and

to make the men under him pay the greatest attention to all Orders, he is not fit for his situaation, and he is to recollect that the safety and honor of his Regiment may frequently depend upon the manner in which he executes his duty.

REPORTS.

18. All Officers in command of Picquets, Patrols, &c., must make written reports of any thing which occurs. There are few occasions when it is necessary to send a verbal report, and it should, if possible, be avoided, as it is very difficult to find Non-commissioned Officers, and Soldiers, who will deliver it correctly. A commander of a Post or Patrol, must be very cautious not to create unnecessary alarms; he must report as fully and as correctly as possible. If he reports the movements of the Enemy, he must recollect that considerable confusion may arise from saying "to the right," or "to the left;" he must say, to *our* right, or to *our* left, or to " the ENEMY's right," or to " the ENEMY's left." If a Non-commissioned Officer cannot send a written report, he must explain the message thoroughly to the Private, and should the latter deliver it incorrectly, he must expect to be punished.

FINIS.

CONTENTS.

SCIENCE OF WAR!
TACTICS
FOR
OFFICERS
OF
INFANTRY, CAVALRY AND ARTILLERY.

ARRANGED AND COMPILED BY
L. v. BUCKHOLTZ.

One Volume, 12mo, Price 75 cts. by mail, post paid.

———

ARMORY, RICHMOND, VA., JAN'Y 8, 1861.

J. W. BANDOLPH—*Dear Sir:*—I have only had time to look over the Military work of Capt. *Buckholtz*, because of my pressing duties, yet I am satisfied that, if printed, much valuable information to our citizen soldiery will be furnished.

The popular works upon military matters, now before the public, are confined to ordinary drills and parades. What is now wanted, is a treatise going to show when the various movements of Artillery, Cavalry, Infantry and Rifle, as taught in their respective drills, should be used in presence of an enemy,—what grounds should be selected for battle and encampment—what precautions to be taking when advancing or retreating—when to act in column—when in line, how to post the different arms to act most favorably—information most essential to success, and without which, no matter how personally brave troops may be, they are exposed to almost certain disaster in presence of an equal number of well drilled and well manœuvered troops, and this information Capt. Buckholtz furnishes in his work.

I have no hesitation in recommending it.

Very respectfully yours,

CHARLES DIMMOCK, Capt., &c., &c.

———

Published and for sale by

J. W. RANDOLPH, RICHMOND, VA.
Also for sale by Booksellers generally.

NEW MILITARY WORK.

ON

INFANTRY CAMP DUTY, FIELD FORTIFICATION, AND COAST DEFENSE.

Prepared and arranged by CAPT. L. v. BUCKHOLTZ, with plates, 16mo. muslin. Price 50 cts. by mail, post paid.

———

RECOMMENDATIONS.

"This is a mere pocket-book in size, but it is crowded with instruction for military men—instruction gathered and condensed from the great bulk of works on military science. It encloses grains of wheat, threshed, as it were, out of the great stack—is simple, convenient and comprehensive. It is from the pen of Captain Buckholtz, of this city, a gentleman who has seen service on the continent of Europe, and who is an accomplished officer."—*Richmond Dispatch*.

"We are always pleased to meet with a Southern Book, one written, printed and bound in our own section by our own people, and we therefore greet with pleasure two military works now before us, by Captain Buckholtz, and published by J. W. Randolph, Richmond.

The first is "*On Infantry Camp Duty, Field Fortification, and Coast Defense.*" Under the head of Infantry Camp Duty we are instructed in out guards, patrols, vanguard. side-guard, rear guard, ambuscade, surprise, and transports. In Field Fortification we have instructions on fortifications, regularly constructed forts, attack and defense, fortresses, and a description of the principal parts of fortified works.

The chapter on Coast Defense is most excellent.

As an elementary work on the subjects treated, this book has no superior, and we commend it to our military.

The second book is, "*Tactics for Officers of Infantry, Cavalry, and Artillery.*" This is a most complete military work, comprising instruction in the three departments of the army, and contains much information which we have never met with in the popular military works of the day."—*Norfolk Southern Argus*.

———

Published and for sale by

J. W. RANDOLPH, RICHMOND, VA.

Also for sale by Booksellers generally.

www.ingramcontent.com/pod-product-compliance
Lightning Source LLC
Chambersburg PA
CBHW021517090426
42739CB00007B/653